AAT Level 4 Diploma in Accounting
Financial Statements

Third edition June 2015

ISBN 9781 4727 2191 4

British Library Cataloguing-in-Publication Data

A catalogue record for this book is available from the British Library

Published by

BPP Learning Media Ltd,
BPP House, Aldine Place,
142-144 Uxbridge Road,
London W12 8AA

www.bpp.com/learningmedia

Printed in the United Kingdom
by Ashford Colour Press Ltd.

Unit 600, Fareham Reach,
Fareham Road, Gosport,
Hampshire, PO13 0FW

Your learning materials, published by BPP Learning Media Ltd, are printed on paper obtained from traceable sustainable sources.

Welcome to BPP Learning Media's AAT **Passcards for Financial Statements**.

- They **save you time**. Important topics are summarised for you.

- They incorporate **diagrams** to kick-start your memory.

- They follow the overall **structure** of the BPP Text, but BPP's AAT **Passcards** are not just a condensed book. Each card has been separately designed for clear presentation. Topics are self contained and can be grasped visually.

- AAT **Passcards** are **just the right size** for pockets, briefcases and bags.

- AAT **Passcards focus on the assessment** you will be facing.

- AAT **Passcards focus on the essential points** that you need to know in the workplace, or when completing your assessment.

Run through the complete set of **Passcards** as often as you can during your final revision period. The day before the assessment, try to go through the **Passcards** again! You will then be well on your way to completing your assessment successfully.

Good luck!

Contents

1: Limited companies

Topic List

The nature of limited companies

The accounts of limited companies

Share capital

Reserves

Loan finance

The Financial Statements paper is concerned with one specific type of business organisation: the limited company.

There are several important ways in which a limited company differs from a sole trader or a partnership.

Limited liability

A limited company gives its owners **limited liability**. The owners' liability is limited to the amount that they have paid for their shares. If the company becomes insolvent, the maximum amount that the owners lose is the amount of capital that they have invested in the company. Investing in a listed company is less risky and therefore more attractive than investing in a partnership or a sole trader. Limited companies may be private (Limited or Ltd) or public (plc).

The purpose of financial statements is to **provide information about financial position and financial performance to those outside the business.**

- Limited companies must publish their annual accounts (Companies Act 2006).
- These must comply with regulations in the CA 2006 and accounting standards and may have to be audited.

- Limited companies may be owned and managed by different people.
- Limited companies are owned by shareholders.
- Shareholders appoint directors to manage business on their behalf.
- There may be a large number of shareholders.
- Shareholders receive a share of profits.

Statement of profit or loss

Prepared in exactly the same way as for a sole trader/partnership, down to net profit.

	£
Revenue	X
Cost of sales	(X)
Gross profit	X
Expenses	(X)
Profit/(loss) before tax	X
Tax	(X)
Profit/(loss) for the period	X

- Limited companies pay **corporation tax** on their profits.
- This is because a limited company has a separate legal personality from its owners; it is taxed as a separate entity.

Statement of financial position

Prepared in exactly the same way as for a sole trader/partnership, with exception of capital/owners' interest.

	£
Assets	X
Equity	
Share capital	X
Reserves	X
	X
Liabilities	X
	X

Share capital

Share capital is the capital invested in a company by its owners. The capital of a company is divided into a number of identifiable units, called shares. When a company is formed, it issues shares, which are purchased by investors. Most shares are **ordinary shares**.

- The nominal value of a share (eg £1, 50p) is decided when the shares are issued. Shares are stated in the statement of financial position at their nominal value.
- The market value of a share is the value at which it is traded on the Stock Exchange. This changes over time and is irrelevant to the financial statements.
- Issued share capital is the nominal amount of share capital that has actually been issued to shareholders.

Ordinary shares	Preference shares
<ul><li>Entitle holders to share in profits (after preference dividend)</li><li>Entitle holders to vote</li><li>If the company wound up, entitle holders to any capital remaining after creditors/preference shareholders have been paid</li><li>Holders are effective owners of company</li><li>Holders bear risks of business</li></ul>	<ul><li>Carry right to fixed rate of dividend</li><li>Do not normally carry voting rights</li><li>If the company wound up, holders have right to repayment of capital before anything paid to ordinary shareholders</li><li>Often treated as a non-current liability in the financial statements, rather than as share capital</li></ul>

Reserves

- Reserves are part of equity and 'belong' to the equity (ordinary) shareholders.
- All limited companies have at least one reserve: retained earnings.
- Retained earnings = profit made to date, less corporation tax and dividends.

Distributable reserves

- Can be paid out as dividends
- Include:
  - Retained earnings
  - Other reserves set aside for specific purpose, eg, general reserve

Non-distributable reserves

- Reserves which the company is legally obliged to set up in certain circumstances
- Cannot be used to pay dividends
- Include:
  - Share premium
  - Revaluation reserve

Dividends

- Profit after tax is available for distribution to the shareholders, in the form of dividends.
- Return on a shareholders' investment; normally expressed as an amount per share.
- Not an expense; therefore not recognised in profit or loss. Instead they are deducted from retained earnings.
- Any profit not distributed as dividends is retained by the company.

Loan finance

A company can raise finance by borrowing: taking out a long-term bank loan or issuing loan stock (sometimes called loan notes or debentures).

Loan stock and other long-term loans differ from share capital as follows:

- Lenders are creditors; shareholders are owners.
- Interest must be paid regardless of the profit/loss made by the company; dividends need not be paid.
- Lenders can take legal action if their interest not paid/loan not repaid on due date.
- Loans normally have a fixed repayment date.

2: The frameworks

This chapter looks at the regulatory framework: the requirements of the Companies Act 2006 and the nature of accounting standards.

It also covers the IASB's Conceptual Framework for Financial Reporting.

Limited companies are required to observe various rules and regulations when preparing financial statements. The main sources of regulation in the UK are:

- Companies legislation (the Companies Act 2006)
- Accounting standards

Requirements of the Companies Act 2006

- The directors must prepare and approve annual accounts and circulate them to the shareholders.
- The accounts must be filed with the Registrar of Companies (ie published).
- Quoted companies must prepare and file IAS accounts (following IFRSs and IASs)
- Other companies prepare either:
  - Companies Act accounts (following UK standards); or
  - IFRS accounts (following IFRSs and IASs).
- Directors have a legal duty to keep adequate accounting records.
- Published accounts must show a **true and fair view** (in IAS 1 called **fair presentation**).

Accounting standards

- Authoritative statements of how particular types of transactions and other events should be reflected in financial statements.

- Fair presentation/true and fair view = compliance with accounting standards.

Two sets of accounting standards:

UK accounting standards:
(FRSs and SSAPs)

International accounting standards:
(IFRSs and IASs)

In your Assessment, you will be expected to prepare financial statements that comply with
International Financial Reporting Standards.

2: The frameworks

International Financial Reporting Standards

Since January 2005, all EU quoted companies, including UK companies, have been required to use international financial reporting standards. Two types are in force:

- International Financial Reporting Standards (IFRSs): issued by the International Accounting Standards Board (IASB) since 2001.

- International Accounting Standards (IASs): issued before 2001 by the IASB's predecessor, the International Accounting Standards Committee (IASC).

The IASB's *Conceptual Framework*

The *Conceptual Framework* sets out the principles and concepts that the IASB believes should underlie the preparation and presentation of financial statements.

It is not an accounting standard.

Objective of financial statements (general purpose financial reporting)

To **provide financial information** about the reporting entity that is **useful** to **existing and potential investors, lenders and other creditors** in **making decisions** about **providing resources** to the entity.

Users of financial statements (general purpose financial reports)

The *Conceptual Framework* states that the most important (primary) users are:

- Investors (existing and potential)
- Lenders and other creditors (existing and potential)

> Financial statements are prepared in order to give them the information that they need

Investors and lenders use financial information to make decisions about buying, selling or holding equity and debt instruments, and providing or setting loans and other forms of credit.

They need information about an entity's

- Economic resources (assets) ⎫
- Claims (liabilities) ⎬ (financial position)
- Changes in economic resources and claims (financial performance)
- Management's efficiency and effectiveness

Underlying assumption: going concern

Financial statements are prepared on the assumption that the entity will continue to operate for the foreseeable future; no intention to liquidate or curtail scale of operations materially.

What makes financial information useful? (Qualitative characteristics)

Fundamental qualitative characteristics

Useful information:

- Is **relevant**: it is capable of making a difference in decisions (includes **materiality**).
- **Faithfully represents** what it purports to represent: it is complete, neutral and free from error.

Enhancing qualitative characteristics

These characteristics enhance the usefulness of information that is relevant and faithfully represented.

- Comparability
- Verifiability
- Timeliness
- Understandability

Materiality

Information is **material** if omitting it or misstating it could influence decisions that users make on the basis of financial information about a specific reporting entity.

'Fair presentation/true and fair view'

- Required by CA 2006 and IFRSs
- No definition in IFRSs or *Conceptual Framework*
- 'True and fair' is legal concept
- Normally given by complying with all applicable regulations eg IFRSs and IASs
- Meaning changes over time as business and generally accepted accounting practice change

The elements of financial statements

- **Asset**: a resource controlled by the entity as a result of past events and from which future economic benefits are expected to flow to the entity.
- **Liability**: a present obligation of the entity arising from past events, the settlement of which is expected to result in an outflow of resources embodying economic benefits from the entity.
- **Equity**: the owners' residual interest in the assets of the entity after deducting all its liabilities.
- **Income**: increases in economic benefits during the accounting period in the form of inflows or enhancement of assets or decreases of liabilities that result in increases in equity, other than those relating to contributions from owners.
- **Expenses**: decreases in economic benefits during the accounting period in the form of outflows or depletions of assets or incurrences of liabilities that result in decreases in equity, other than those relating to distributions to owners.
- **Contributions from owners**: increases in equity resulting from transfers from owners in their capacity as owners (eg issues of share capital).
- **Distributions to owners**: decreases in equity resulting from transfers to owners in their capacity as owners (eg dividends).

The elements and the accounting equation

ASSETS – LIABILITIES = EQUITY

EQUITY = CONTRIBUTIONS FROM OWNERS + INCOME – EXPENSES – DISTRIBUTIONS TO OWNERS

Recognising the elements of financial statements

An item that meets the definition of an element (eg an asset or a liability) should be recognised if:

- It is probable that any future economic benefit associated with the item will flow to or from the entity; and
- The item has a cost or value that can be measured with reliability.

Recognition and the accounting equation

- If net assets increase, income or a gain is recognised; and
- If net assets are reduced or eliminated, an expense or a loss is recognised.

    CLOSING NET ASSETS – OPENING NET ASSETS = PROFIT/LOSS FOR THE PERIOD

Measuring the elements of financial statements

Measurement is the process of determining the monetary amounts at which items are recognised and carried in the financial statements.

Possible measurement bases:

- **Historic cost**: cost at acquisition
- **Current cost**
- **Realisable value**: selling price
- **Present value**: value of future cash flows adjusted for time value of money

Historic cost is the most common way of measuring items, but may be combined with others, eg inventories carried at lower of cost and net realisable value.

Notes

3: The statement of financial position

Topic List

Presentation of financial statements

The statement of financial position

IAS 1 Presentation of Financial Statements *sets out general requirements for the presentation of financial statements, including the form and structure of the main financial statements.*

This chapter concentrates on the statement of financial position.

Make sure that you practise drafting financial statements; attempt as many assessment tasks as possible.

Components of financial statements

IAS 1 states that a complete set of financial statements comprises:

- A statement of financial position as at the end of the period
- A statement of profit or loss and other comprehensive income for the period
- A statement of changes in equity for the period
- A statement of cash flows for the period
- Notes

Financial statements should be prepared at least annually.

Fair presentation

Financial statements must present fairly the financial position, financial performance and cash flows of an entity. This is achieved by:

- Faithful representation of the effects of transactions/events according to definitions and recognition criteria for assets, liabilities, income and expenses in the *Conceptual Framework*.
- Compliance with IFRSs.

Accounting principles

Going concern

Financial statements must be prepared on a going concern basis, unless the entity is not a going concern.

Accruals

Financial statements must be prepared on the accruals basis, except for cash flow information.

Materiality and aggregation

- Each material class of similar items must be presented separately.
- Items that are dissimilar must be presented separately. They cannot be aggregated unless they are individually immaterial.

Offset

Assets and liabilities, and income and expenses, should not be offset unless this is required or permitted by a standard.

Consistency of presentation

An entity must present and classify items in the same way from one period to the next unless:

- There has been a significant change in the entity's operations; or
- A new IFRS requires a different presentation.

Format of the statement of financial position

ASSETS = EQUITY + LIABILITIES

In the Assessment, you will be expected to draft the statement of financial position in a similar format.

Statement of financial position as at

	£'000
Assets	
Non-current assets	
Intangible assets	X
Property, plant and equipment	X
	X
Current assets	
Inventories	X
Trade and other receivables	X
Cash and cash equivalents	X
	X
Total assets	X

The line items should be analysed further, where this is necessary.

Example: property, plant and equipment broken down into:

- Land and buildings
- Plant and machinery
- Motor vehicles

This is normally done in the notes.

Equity and liabilities
Equity
Share capital   X
Share premium   X
Revaluation reserve   X
Retained earnings   X

Total equity   X

Non-current liabilities
Bank loans   X
Long-term provisions   X
                                                 X

Current liabilities
Trade and other payables   X
Tax liabilities   X
Bank overdrafts and loans   X
                                                 X

Total liabilities   X

Total equity and liabilities   X

IAS 1 specifies the line items to be disclosed.

Present additional line items, headings and subtotals if this helps users to understand the information.

Classify assets and liabilities as either current or non-current; present these categories separately (see next section for definitions).

Current and non-current assets and liabilities

These must be classified and presented separately in the statement of financial position.

Current asset

- Entity expects to receive/sell/consume it in normal operating cycle; or
- Held primarily for trading; or
- Expected to be realised within twelve months after the year-end; or
- Cash or a cash equivalent.

Current liability

- Entity expects to settle it in its normal operating cycle; or
- Held primarily for trading; or
- Due to be settled within twelve months after the year-end; or
- Entity does not have the unconditional right to delay settling it for at least twelve months after the year-end.

All other assets and liabilities are non-current.

4: The statements of financial performance

Topic List

The statement of profit or loss and other comprehensive income

The statement of changes in equity

The financial statements

This chapter concentrates on the statement of profit or loss and other comprehensive income and the statement of changes in equity.

As with the statement of financial position, you should practise drafting these statements by attempting as many assessment tasks as possible.

Format

Statement of profit or loss and other comprehensive income for the year ended

IAS 1 specifies the line items to be disclosed.

	£'000
Revenue	X
Cost of sales	(X)
Gross profit	X
Distribution costs	(X)
Administrative expenses	(X)
Profit/(loss) from operations	X
Finance costs	(X)
Profit/(loss) before tax	X
Tax	(X)
Profit/(loss) for the period from continuing operations	**X**

Costs of selling and delivering items to customers, eg sales commissions, delivery costs.

Eg rent and rates, light and heat, office salaries, telephone, postage

Interest payable.

Large/unusual items disclosed separately in notes or as a line item if very significant; eg gain/loss on disposal of assets.

Depreciation may be included under any/all of these headings, read the information carefully.

Other comprehensive income for the period:

£'000

Gains on property revaluation

 X

Total comprehensive income for the period

X

> All items of income and expense for period should be included in profit or loss unless another standard requires otherwise.

> Must be line item for each component of other comprehensive income (only gain/loss on revaluation in Assessment).

> **In the Assessment, you will be asked to draft a single statement of profit or loss and other comprehensive income in a similar format to the one above.**

IAS 1 also allows an entity to present two separate statements:

- A statement of profit or loss; and
- A statement of comprehensive income (showing profit/loss and other comprehensive income).

4: The statements of financial performance

Example of a statement of changes in equity

Statement of changes in equity for the year ended

	Share capital	Other reserves	Retained earnings	Total equity
	£'000	£'000	£'000	£'000
Balance at beginning of year	X	X	X	X
Changes in equity for the year				
Total comprehensive income		X	X	X
Dividends			(X)	(X)
Issue of share capital	X	X		X
Balance at end of year	X	X	X	X

4: The statements of financial performance

The financial statements

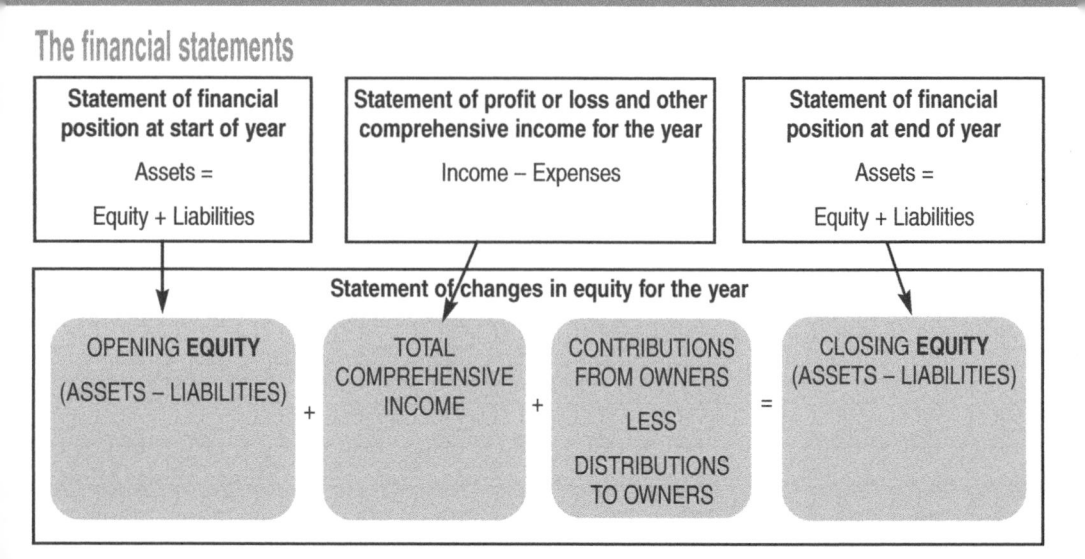

5: The statement of cash flows

IAS 7 requires all entities to present a statement of cash flows.

In the Assessment, there is a good chance that at least one of the tasks will involve drafting a statement of cash flows and a reconciliation of profit from operations to net cash from operating activities. As usual, it is vital that you practise doing this.

A statement of cash flows summarises all movements of cash into and out of a business during the accounting period. This provides users of the financial statements with information about an entity's ability to generate cash and cash equivalents.

Definitions

Cash

Cash on hand and demand deposits.

(Normally includes current account, petty cash, bank overdraft.)

Cash equivalents

Short-term, highly liquid investments that are readily convertible to known amounts of cash and which are subject to an insignificant risk of changes in value.

(Examples: deposit accounts and investments that mature within three months of acquisition.)

Cash flows

Inflows and outflows of cash and cash equivalents.

Cash flows are grouped under headings

Operating activities

The principal revenue producing activities of the entity and other activities that are not investing or financing activities. (IAS 7)

IAS 7 allows two methods of presenting cash flows from operating activities.

Indirect method

Reconcile profit from operations to net cash from operating activities.

Most entities use this method.

Direct method

List and total actual cash flows.

Investing activities

The acquisition and disposal of long-term assets and other investments not included in cash equivalents. (IAS 7)

Financing activities

Activities that result in changes in the size and composition of the contributed equity (share capital) and borrowings of the entity. (IAS 7)

Format of the statement of cash flows (indirect method)

Reconciliation of profit from operations to net cash from operating activities for the year ended

	£'000
Profit from operations	X
Adjustments for:	
Depreciation	X
Dividends received	(X)
(Gain)/loss on disposal of property, plant and equipment	(X)
(Increase)/decrease in inventories	X
(Increase)/decrease in trade and other receivables	(X)
Increase/(decrease) in trade payables	(X)
Cash generated from operations	X
Interest paid	(X)
Tax paid	(X)
Net cash from operating activities	X

Direct method shows:

	£'000
Cash received from customers	X
Cash payments to suppliers and employees	(X)
Cash generated from operations	X
Interest paid	(X)
Tax paid	(X)
Net cash from operating activities	X

Statement of cash flows for the year ended

	£'000	£'000
Net cash from operating activities		X
Investing activities		
Purchase of property, plant and equipment	(X)	
Proceeds on disposal of property, plant and equipment	X	
Interest received	X	
Dividends received	<u>X</u>	
Net cash used in investing activities		(X)
Financing activities		
Proceeds from issue of share capital	X	
Increase in bank loans	X	
Dividends paid	<u>(X)</u>	
Net cash used in financing activities		<u>(X)</u>
Net increase in cash and cash equivalents		X
Cash and cash equivalents at beginning of year		<u>X</u>
Cash and cash equivalents at end of year		<u><u>X</u></u>

Cash generated from operations	<ul><li>Start with profit from operations</li><li>Add back depreciation</li><li>Deduct dividends received (if any). These should be included in investing activities</li><li>Disposal of assets: add back a loss; deduct a gain</li><li>Deduct increase in inventories/trade receivables (decrease in cash)</li><li>Add back increase in payables (increase in cash)</li></ul>
Interest and tax	<ul><li>Interest: if no accruals, interest charge = cash outflow</li><li>Tax: if expense = closing payable, cash outflow = opening payable</li><li>Otherwise: opening balance + charge for year − closing balance = cash outflow</li></ul>
Investing activities	<ul><li>Calculate purchase of PPE: opening balance − disposals − depreciation − closing balance = cash outflow</li><li>Calculate proceeds on disposal from carrying amount and profit/loss on disposal</li><li>Include dividends received (if any)</li></ul>
Financing activities	<ul><li>Cash flow is normally the difference between opening and closing figures in statement of financial position (share capital and share premium, loans)</li><li>Dividends usually given in task; otherwise reconstruct movements in retained earnings</li></ul>
Cash and cash equivalents	<ul><li>Net increase/decrease should equal difference between closing and opening figures in statement of financial position</li></ul>

Advantages

- Can alert users to liquidity problems
- Shows how well (or badly) profit is converted to cash
- Cash is a matter of fact and not easily manipulated
- Not affected by accounting policies or estimates
- Can help users to predict future cash flows
- Easier to understand than profit for some users
- Standard headings enable users to compare cash flows of different entities

Limitations

- Cash balances can be manipulated (eg by delaying payment to suppliers)
- It is possible to focus on cash flow at the expense of profit (eg by not replacing plant and equipment); in the long term a business needs both to survive
- Historical information is not necessarily a reliable indicator of future cash flows

Interpreting the statement of cash flows

- Has cash increased or decreased in the period?
- How material is the increase/decrease in cash compared with the entity's cash balances?
- Does the entity have a positive cash balance or an overdraft?
- Have inventories, receivables and payables increased or decreased?
- Is there enough cash to cover interest, tax and dividends?
- If there has been capital expenditure, where has the cash come from?
- Is debt increasing or decreasing?
- Will the entity be able to pay its debt interest?
- Will the entity be able to repay the debt (if it falls due in the near future)?
- Is the entity likely to need additional long term finance?

6: Property, plant and equipment

Topic List

Recognition

Measurement

Depreciation and disposals

Disclosure

In this chapter we cover the accounting treatment of property, plant and equipment (tangible non-current assets).

You will need to be able to make accounting adjustments, particularly for depreciation, revaluations and disposals of property, plant and equipment. You will also need to learn and understand the main requirements of IAS 16 Property, Plant and Equipment.

Property, plant and equipment

Property, plant and equipment are tangible items that:

- Are held for use in the production or supply of goods or services, for rental to others, or for administrative purposes; and
- Are expected to be used during more than one period.

Examples: land, buildings, machinery, computers, motor vehicles and office furniture.

Recognition

Recognise an item only if:

- It is probable that future economic benefits will flow to the entity; and
- The cost of the item can be measured reliably.

Measurement at recognition

At cost:

- Purchase price; plus
- Any further costs **directly attributable** to bringing the item to location and condition necessary for its intended use.

Includes: delivery costs, assembly costs, professional fees (eg legal), cost of testing asset

Does not include: administrative expenses, cost of staff training to use asset.

Subsequent expenditure

Only include in cost of an item if it will probably result in future economic benefit to entity (by improving performance).

Do not include servicing costs, eg repairs and maintenance; these are an expense.

Measurement after recognition

Choice between

Cost model

(Historic) cost less accumulated depreciation and any accumulated impairment losses.

Revaluation gains

Not normally recognised in profit or loss but part of other comprehensive income.

DEBIT   Cost: fair value – original cost
DEBIT   Accumulated depreciation: total depreciation to date
CREDIT Revaluation reserve: revalued amount (fair value) – carrying amount based on original cost

Revaluation losses

Recognise immediately in profit or loss (if asset previously measured at cost).

Revaluation model

Fair value less any subsequent accumulated depreciation and subsequent impairment losses.

- Fair value: the price that would be received to sell an asset in an orderly transaction between market participants at the measurement date.

- Fair value is normally market value.

- If chosen, must apply to whole class of assets; eg can revalue properties and keep other assets at cost; but cannot revalue some properties and not others.

- Revaluations should be made with sufficient regularity to ensure that carrying amount not materially different from fair value at year-end.

Depreciation and derecognition

All items of property, plant and equipment must be depreciated over their useful lives. The only exception is land; it normally has an indefinite life.

Basic rules

- Recognise depreciation charge for each period in profit or loss.
- Allocate the depreciable amount of an asset on a systematic basis over its useful life.
- **Depreciable amount** = cost/fair value − residual value (ie where an asset has been revalued, charge is based on fair value).
- **Residual amount** is estimated amount that entity would currently obtain from disposal at end of asset's useful life.
- No depreciation method prescribed in IAS 16, but should reflect pattern in which asset's future economic benefits expected to be consumed.

Review of depreciation charge

At each year-end (as a minimum) review:

- Depreciation method
- Residual value
- Useful life

If change required, treat as **change in accounting estimate**, for example:

- (If method changed) depreciate using new method over remaining useful life.
- (If useful life changed) depreciate carrying amount of asset over revised useful life.

Disposals and derecognition

Derecognise an item:

- On disposal; or
- When no future economic benefits are expected from its use or disposal.

Gain or loss on disposal/derecognition:

- Calculate as net sale proceeds (if any) less carrying amount (whether based on original cost or on fair value).
- Recognise in profit or loss for period.

Disclosure	*Land and buildings* £'000	*Plant and machinery* £'000	*Motor vehicles* £'000	*Total* £'000
Cost (or valuation)				
At beginning of year	X	X	X	X
Additions	X	X	–	X
Revaluation	X	–	–	X
Disposals	(X)	(X)	(X)	(X)
At end of year	X	X	X	X
Depreciation				
At beginning of year	X	X	X	X
Charge for year	X	X	X	X
Revaluation	(X)	–	–	(X)
Disposals	(X)	(X)	(X)	(X)
At end of year	X	X	X	X
Net carrying amount				
At end of year	X	X	X	X
At beginning of year	X	X	X	X

This is a pro-forma note showing information required by IAS 16

Also disclose:

- Measurement bases (ie cost or fair value)
- Depreciation methods
- Useful lives

7: Intangible assets and inventories

Topic List

Intangible assets (IAS 38)

Impairment of assets (IAS 36)

Inventories (IAS 2)

In this chapter we cover intangible assets (including research and development expenditure), impairment of assets and inventories.

Intangible assets

An **intangible asset** is an identifiable non-monetary asset without physical substance.

Examples: brand names; technical knowledge; licences; patents; publishing titles; trademarks; goodwill; development expenditure.

General principles

- To be **identifiable**, an asset must either be **separable** from the rest of the business or must arise from **contractual or other legal rights.**

- Recognise an intangible asset only when:
  - Probable that future economic benefits will flow to the entity; and
  - Cost can be measured reliably.

- On initial recognition, measure at **cost** (ie all directly attributable costs necessary to create/produce asset to operate in intended manner).

Goodwill

If a business has goodwill the value of the business as a whole is greater than the total value of its individual assets and liabilities.

Internally generated goodwill

- Goodwill that a business generates over time (eg through reputation, technical know how of staff etc).

- Never recognised as an asset (IAS 38 forbids); Reason: cannot be measured reliably.

Purchased goodwill

- Difference between the cost of an acquired entity and the total fair values of its identifiable assets and liabilities.

- Has a cost to the business that acquired it; this is reflected in purchase price.

- Therefore can be measured reliably at the time of purchase transaction.

- Recognise as an asset in statement of financial position.

See also Chapters 9 and 10 on group accounts.

IAS 38 also forbids recognition of other internally generated intangible assets: eg brands, mastheads, publishing titles, customer lists.

7: Intangible assets and inventories

Research and development expenditure

Research

Recognise expense in profit or loss when incurred.

Development

Recognise an intangible asset (ie capitalise expenditure) if entity can demonstrate that project meets **all six** criteria; otherwise charge to profit or loss when incurred.

- **Technical feasibility** of completing the asset.
- **Intention to complete** the asset.
- **Ability to use or sell** the asset.
- **How** the asset will **generate probable future economic benefits.**
- **Availability of adequate** technical, financial and other **resources** to complete development.
- Ability to **measure reliably** the expenditure attributable to the asset during its development.

Amortisation and impairment

- Useful life of an intangible asset can be finite or indefinite.

- If finite, amortise over useful life (same principle as depreciation for tangible assets).

- If indefinite, do not amortise, but review at least annually for evidence of impairment (see next section).

- Also review useful life annually; if no longer indefinite, treat change as change in accounting estimate.

Impairment of assets

Impairment is a reduction in the recoverable amount of an asset below its carrying amount.

An **impairment loss** is the amount by which the carrying amount of an asset exceeds its recoverable amount.

Carry out an impairment review when:

- Indication that impairment has occurred

Examples:

- Significant decline in asset's market value
- Obsolescence or physical damage
- Significant adverse change in business or market
- Significant change in the way in which asset is used
- Operating losses/net cash outflows for asset expected

Annual impairment reviews required for:

- Intangible assets with an indefinite useful life
- Goodwill acquired in a business combination (see Chapter 9)

Carrying out an impairment review

An asset should be measured
at the **lower** of:

Carrying amount ← → Recoverable amount

Higher of

Fair value less costs of disposal ← → Value in use

- **Carrying amount**: amount at which asset is recognised less any accumulated depreciation (amortisation)/accumulated impairment losses.

- **Fair value less costs of disposal**: the price that would be received to sell an asset in an orderly transaction between market participants at the measurement date, less the costs of disposal.

- **Value in use**: the present value of future cash flows expected to be obtained from asset.

- If carrying amount is **greater than** recoverable amount, the asset is impaired
- Carrying amount – recoverable amount = **impairment loss**

Accounting for impairment losses

If asset carried at **original cost**:

- Recognise immediately in profit or loss.

If asset has been **revalued** above cost:

- Treat as downward revaluation.
- Recognise in other comprehensive income (set against revaluation surplus).
- If recoverable amount is less than depreciated historic cost, recognise difference in profit or loss.

- Review remaining useful life and revise if necessary.
- Depreciate revised carrying amount over new estimate of remaining useful life.

Inventories

Inventories are assets:

- Held for sale in the ordinary course of business
- In the process of production for such sale; or
- In the form of materials or supplies to be consumed in the production process or in the rendering of services.

> **Inventories should be measured at the lower of cost and net realisable value.**
>
> Comparison between cost and net realisable value must be made for each individual item, or each group of similar items, not for inventories as a whole.

Cost comprises all costs of purchase, costs of conversion and other costs incurred in bringing the inventories to their present location and condition.

(Do **not** include: abnormal production costs, administrative overheads, selling costs)

Net realisable value is the estimated selling price in the ordinary course of business less the estimated costs of completion; and the estimated costs necessary to make the sale.

Methods of arriving at purchase cost

- Actual cost (use where items not ordinarily interchangeable)
- First in first out (FIFO)
- ~~Last in first out (LIFO)~~   NOT ALLOWED
- Weighted average cost (AVCO)

Use same method for all inventories having a similar nature and use.

8: Further accounting standards

This chapter looks at the accounting treatment of corporation tax in the financial statements.

It also covers a number of other topics: accounting for leases; provisions, contingent liabilities and contingent assets; events after the reporting period; and revenue recognition.

Make sure that you understand the main principles of each of the accounting standards.

Corporation tax

Statement of profit or loss and other comprehensive income

The tax expense (in profit or loss) for the year consists of:

	£
Charge for current year	X
Adjustment in respect of prior period	X/(X)
	X

Statement of financial position (extract)

	£
Current liabilities:	
Tax liability	X

Charge for current year: an estimate of the tax payable on profits for the year.

Adjustment in respect of prior period: required because the amount that is actually agreed with and paid to HMRC after the year-end is usually different from the estimate.

Unpaid corporation tax is a **current liability**; usually = the estimated charge for the current year in profit or loss.

To recognise the estimated corporation tax charge for the year:

DEBIT Tax expense (profit or loss)

CREDIT Tax payable (current liability)

Leases

Finance lease

Transfers substantially all the risks and rewards of ownership of an asset to the lessee.

Operating lease

A lease other than a finance lease.

Indications that a lease is a finance lease:

- It transfers ownership of the asset to the lessee by the end of the lease term
- It is for all or most of the asset's useful life
- At the start, the present value of the minimum lease payments is at least substantially all of the fair value of the leased asset
- The asset is specialised

Accounting for an operating lease

- Charge lease payments to profit or loss (normally) on a straight line basis over the lease term

Accounting for a finance lease

At the start of the lease	Recognise leased **asset**	Recognise **liability** for lease payments
	Measure asset and liability at same amount	
Over the term of the lease	Depreciate asset over useful life (charge to profit or loss)	Add interest to liability(finance cost in profit or loss)
		Deduct lease payments from liability

Statement of financial position

Non-current assets

Cost	X
Depreciation	(X)
Net carrying amount	X

Non-current liabilities

Finance lease obligation	X

Current liabilities

Finance lease obligation	X

Statement of profit or loss and other comprehensive income (profit or loss)

Depreciation expense	X
Finance costs	X

Provisions

A **provision** is a liability of uncertain timing or amount (IAS 37).

A **liability** is a present obligation arising from past events, the settlement of which is expected to result in an outflow of resources embodying economic benefits (IAS 37 and IASB *Conceptual Framework*).

Recognition

Only recognise a provision when:

- An entity has a **present obligation** as a result of a past event; and

- It is **probable** that an outflow of resources embodying economic benefits will be required to settle the obligation; and

- A **reliable** estimate can be made of the **amount** of the obligation.

Measurement

Measure a provision at the **best estimate** of the expenditure required to **settle the obligation at the year-end**.

Contingent liability

Definition:

- A **possible obligation** that arises from past events and whose existence will be confirmed only by the occurrence of one or more uncertain future events; or

- A present obligation that is not recognised.

Do not recognise.

Disclose unless the possibility of a transfer of economic benefits to settle it is remote.

Contingent asset

Definition:

- A **possible asset** that arises from past events and whose existence will be confirmed only by the occurrence of one or more uncertain future events.

Do not recognise.

Disclose if an inflow of economic benefits is probable.

Events after the reporting period

Events after the reporting period: those events, both favourable and unfavourable, which occur between the end of the reporting period and the date on which the financial statements are authorised for issue.

Adjusting events: events which provide evidence of conditions that existed at the end of the reporting period.

Non adjusting events: events which are indicative of conditions which arose after the reporting period.

Examples:
Evidence of impairment of assets
Insolvency of a customer

Examples:
Loss of assets due to fire or flood
Purchase or sale of assets

Financial statements are prepared on the basis of conditions at the year-end

Adjust the financial statements.

(If material) **disclose** nature of event and an estimate of the financial effect in a note.

Revenue

Revenue is the gross inflow of economic benefits (eg cash, receivables) arising in the course of the **ordinary activities** of the entity. (IAS 18)

Revenue is measured at the **fair value** of the consideration received or receivable (often the cash received/receivable).

Revenue from sale of goods

Recognise when all the following conditions are satisfied:

- Entity has transferred the significant risks and rewards of ownership to buyer.

- Entity retains neither continuing managerial involvement nor effective control over the goods.

- Amount of revenue can be measured reliably.

- It is probable that economic benefits will flow to the entity.

- Costs of transaction can be measured reliably.

Revenue from rendering of services

Recognise by reference to the stage of completion of the transaction at the year-end, if outcome can be estimated reliably. Similar conditions to revenue from sale of goods.

Dividend income

Recognise when:

- Normal criteria met (probable economic benefits + reliable measurement); and

- Shareholder's right to receive payment is established.

Notes

9: Group accounts: the consolidated statement of financial position

Topic List

Groups

The consolidated statement of financial position

Intra-group adjustments

If a company (the parent) controls another company (its subsidiary), it must prepare consolidated financial statements.

It is virtually certain that one of the tasks in your Assessment will involve drafting either a consolidated statement of financial position, a consolidated statement of profit or loss, or both. Adopt a logical approach and practise as much as possible.

Groups	The consolidated statement of financial position	Intra-group adjustments

A **group** of companies consists of a **parent (holding) company** and all its **subsidiaries**.

Although the individual companies within the group are separate legal entities, the parent and the subsidiary operate as a **single economic entity**: the **group**.

Definitions (IFRS 10)

A **parent** is an entity that controls one or more entities (subsidiaries).

A **subsidiary** is an entity that is **controlled** by another entity (the parent).

Consolidated financial statements are the financial statements of a group in which the assets, liabilities, equity, income and expenses of the parent and its subsidiaries are presented as those of a single economic entity.

An investor **controls** an investee when the investor is exposed, or has rights, to variable returns from its involvement with the investee and has the ability to affect those returns through its **power** over the investee.

An entity is a subsidiary if the parent controls it.

Control

An investor controls an investee if and only if the investor has **all** the following:

- **Power** over the investee;
- Exposure, or rights, to **variable returns** from its involvement with the investee; and
- The ability to **use its power** over the investee to **affect the amount** of the investor's returns.

Power

An investor has **power** over an investee when it has existing **rights** that give it the current ability to direct its relevant activities (usually its normal trading activities).

The most common form of rights that give power are **voting rights** where an investor holds equity shares in another entity.

In the Assessment, you can normally assume that control exists where an investor (the parent) owns 50% or more of the voting power of an investee (the subsidiary), unless you are told otherwise.

Basic consolidation step-by-step

Step 1   Establish the group structure

> For the purpose of this illustration, we assume that P plc owns 80% of S Ltd

Step 2   Calculate goodwill

	£'000	£'000
Cost of investment/price paid		X
Less S Ltd's net assets acquired		
Share capital × 80%	X	
Retained earnings × 80%	X	
Fair value adjustments (if any) × 80%	X	
		(X)
Goodwill on acquisition		X
Less: impairment		(X)
		X

Goodwill: an asset representing the future economic benefits arising from other assets acquired in a business combination that are not individually identified and separately recognised (IFRS 3).

- Recognise as an intangible asset in consolidated statement of financial position.
- Measure at cost less any impairment losses (no amortisation).
- Test for impairment annually.

Step 3   **Calculate the consolidated retained earnings reserve**

	£'000	£'000
P plc		X
S Ltd: At year-end	X	
Less: At acquisition	(X)	
Group share (80%)	X	X
		X
Less: impairment of goodwill		(X)
		X

> Consolidated reserves only include S Ltd's post-acquisition profits.
>
> S Ltd's pre- acquisition profits are excluded from the consolidated retained earnings reserve.

Step 4   **Calculate non-controlling interest**

	£'000
Share capital of S Ltd at year-end × 20%	X
Retained earnings of S Ltd at year-end × 20%	X
Fair value adjustments (if any) × 20%	X
Non-controlling interest	X

> **Non-controlling interest:** the equity in a subsidiary not attributable to the parent (IFRS 3).
>
> In the Assessment, it will always be calculated as the portion of S Ltd's net assets **not** owned by P plc.

Step 5 Add together the assets and liabilities of P plc and S Ltd
Consolidated statement of financial position as at

£'000

The consolidated statement of financial position includes 100% of the subsidiary's individual assets and liabilities. The parent controls 100% of these, even though it only owns 80%.

ASSETS
Non-current assets
Intangible assets: goodwill   X
Other non-current assets (P + 100% S)   X
   X
Current assets (P + 100% S)   X
   X

EQUITY AND LIABILITIES
Equity
Share capital (P only)   X
Retained earnings (P + 80% S post-acquisition)   X
   X

The sub-total below retained earnings shows the equity that 'belongs' to the parent.

Non-controlling interest (20% S net assets at year-end)   X

The non-controlling interest in the net assets of the subsidiary is shown on a separate line within equity.

Total equity   X
Total liabilities (P + 100% S)   X
   X

Fair value adjustments

IFRS 3 states that the identifiable assets and liabilities of a subsidiary that are acquired by a parent should be recognised in the consolidated financial statements at their **fair values** at the date of the acquisition.

- **Fair value** is the price that would be received to sell an asset or paid to transfer a liability in an orderly transaction between market participants at the measurement date.

- The **goodwill calculation** is based on the **fair values** of the subsidiary's **identifiable** net assets **at acquisition date**.

- Therefore, may need to adjust assets to fair value before consolidation (see pro-forma workings above).

- May also need to recognise additional assets/liabilities (eg subsidiary's internally generated intangibles and/or contingent liabilities).

- A gain on a bargain purchase (negative goodwill) is recognised immediately as a **gain** in profit or loss (this is **rare**).

Intra-group sales

If one group company has sold goods to another at a profit and the goods remain in inventory at the year-end, both inventory and profit are **overstated** from the perspective of the **group**.

- Calculate the amount of unrealised profit
- Adjust the consolidated statement of financial position

Sales from P to S (P has made profit)
DEBIT Consolidated retained earnings
CREDIT Inventories

Sales from S to P (S has made profit, so need to apportion between group and NCI)
DEBIT Consolidated retained earnings (group share)
DEBIT Non-controlling interest (NCI share)
CREDIT Inventories

Intra-group balances

Cancel out any trade receivables and trade payables against each other.

10: Group accounts: further aspects

Topic List

The consolidated statement of profit or loss

Further points

Associates

This chapter covers the preparation of the consolidated statement of profit or loss. You should pay particular attention to the treatment of intra-group transactions.

Basic consolidation step-by-step

Step 1   Establish the group structure.

> For the purpose of this illustration, we assume that P plc owns 80% of S Ltd

Step 2   Add together the statements of the parent and the subsidiary, line by line, from revenue to profit for the year.

- Adjust revenue and cost of sales for any intra-group sales/purchases (see below)

Step 3   Calculate non-controlling interest.

	£'000
NCI % × S Ltd's profit for the year	X

- If S Ltd has sold goods to P plc during year, need to adjust for any unrealised profit made by S Ltd (see below)

Consolidated statement of profit or loss for the year ended

	£'000
Revenue (P + 100% S − intra-group sales)	X
Cost of sales (P + 100% S − intra-group sales + unrealised profit)	(X)
Gross profit	X
Operating expenses (P + 100% S)	(X)
Profit from operations	X
Finance costs (P + 100% S)	(X)
Profit before tax	X
Tax (P + 100% S)	(X)
Profit for the period from continuing operations	X
Attributable to:	
Equity holders of the parent (P + 80% S profit for year)	X
Non-controlling interest (20% S profit for year)	X
	X

P **controls** 100% of S's results, even though it only owns 80%.

Any impairment loss on goodwill for year normally in administrative expenses.

Profit for the year is split between profits owned by the non-controlling interest and profits owned by the group.

Intra-group sales

Where one company sells goods to another during the year:

- Intra-group sales and purchases are cancelled against each other; and
- Any unrealised profit is added to cost of sales (it reduces closing inventories)

To cancel an intra-group sale:

DEBIT (reduce) Revenue
CREDIT (reduce) Cost of sales
by the total amount of the intra-group sale

To eliminate unrealised profit:

Sales from P to S (P has made profit)

Increase cost of sales (100% unrealised profit)

Sales from S to P (S has made profit, so need to apportion between group and NCI)

Increase cost of sales (100% unrealised profit)

Calculate non-controlling interest as:

NCI% × S profit for the year	X
NCI% × unrealised profit	(X)
	$\overline{\overline{X}}$

Consolidated financial statements must include **all** subsidiaries of the parent.

Consolidated financial statements must be prepared using uniform accounting policies for similar transactions and other events in similar circumstances.

Must adjust before consolidation if a subsidiary uses different accounting policies from the parent.

Associates

An **associate** is an entity over which the investor has significant influence (IAS 28).

Significant influence is the power to participate in the financial and operating policy decisions of the investee but is not control or joint control over those policies.

- Significant influence presumed if **20% or more** of voting power held

- No significant influence presumed if less than 20% of voting power held

Usually significant influence if:

- Investor is represented on the board of directors

- Investor takes part in policy making processes

- Material transactions between the entities

A holding of between 20% and 50% normally gives significant influence but not control.

IAS 28 states that the **equity method** should be used.

Consolidated statement of financial position	Consolidated statement of profit or loss
■ Include investment in associate in non-current assets (separate line item)	■ Include investor's (group's) share of associate's profit after tax as a separate line item above profit before tax
■ Calculate as:	
– Cost; plus	
– Investor's (group's) share of associate's post acquisition profits/losses	
■ Alternative calculation:	
– Investor's (group's) share of net assets; plus goodwill on acquisition	

Notes

11: Interpreting financial statements

Topic List

Overview

Profitability

Liquidity and use of resources

Financial position

Limitations of ratio analysis

This chapter concentrates on ratio analysis, a technique for analysing and interpreting the information in financial statements.

As well as learning the calculations, it is essential that you are able to interpret and evaluate changes in the ratios and identify possible reasons for these.

The main objective of financial statements is to help users make economic decisions.

Users external to a business need to interpret its financial statements to understand its financial performance (profitability) and financial position, liquidity and use of resources.

In the Assessment you may be asked to:

- Calculate ratios
- Compare a set of ratios with:
    - Ratios of the previous accounting period for the same company; or
    - Ratios of another company; or
    - Industry average ratios.
- Comment on specific ratios; not only whether a ratio has improved/deteriorated, but possible reasons **why**.
- Suggest ways in which particular ratios could be improved.
- Write a report, letter or email; ask yourself:
    - Who is the interpretation for?
    - What are they most interested in?
    - What decision do they need to make?

Return on capital employed

$$\text{Return on capital employed (ROCE)} = \frac{\text{Profit from operations}}{\text{Total equity} + \text{Non-current liabilities}} \times 100\%$$

ROCE measures the total return made by the company on both loans (debt capital) and share capital. It judges profits earned in relation to the resources available.

ROCE depends on two things:

- Profitability (see operating profit percentage)
- Use of resources/assets (see asset turnover)

$$\frac{\text{Profit from operations}}{\text{Total equity} + \text{Non-current liabilities}} = \frac{\text{Profit from operations}}{\text{Revenue}} \times \frac{\text{Revenue}}{\text{Total assets} - \text{Current liabilities}}$$

Variation

Return on shareholders' funds $= \dfrac{\text{Profit after tax}}{\text{Total equity}} \times 100\%$	Measures return to ordinary shareholders on their investment (return on equity only, excluding debt finance)

Profit percentages and expense ratios

Operating profit percentage (net profit margin) $= \dfrac{\text{Profit from operations}}{\text{Revenue}} \times 100\%$ Gross profit percentage $= \dfrac{\text{Gross profit}}{\text{Revenue}} \times 100\%$	Measures the overall profitability of a business

The **expense/revenue percentage** can be calculated for operating expenses in total or for a specific expense:

$$\text{Expense/revenue percentage} = \frac{\text{Operating expenses}}{\text{Revenue}} \text{ or } \frac{\text{Specific expense}}{\text{Revenue}} \times 100\%$$

A high expenses ratio normally = a low operating profit percentage.

Asset turnover

$$\text{Asset turnover} = \frac{\text{Revenue}}{\text{Total assets} - \text{Current liabilities}} \text{ or } \frac{\text{Revenue}}{\text{Non-current assets}}$$

Measures the efficiency with which a business uses its resources to generate sales (revenue generated by each £1 of assets). The higher the number, the more efficient the business.

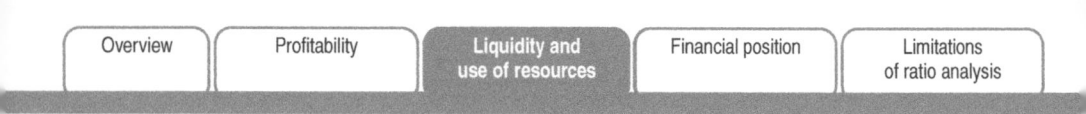

Liquidity

Liquidity ratios show whether a business is likely to be able to meet its debts as they fall due.

Current ratio $= \dfrac{\text{Current assets}}{\text{Current liabilities}}$	Shows the extent to which current liabilities are covered by cash or other current assets
Quick ratio $= \dfrac{\text{Current assets} - \text{Inventories}}{\text{Current liabilities}}$	Measures immediate solvency of a business. Excludes inventories; these cannot be converted into cash quickly

The ratios below measure the ability of a business to control its **working capital** and to use it efficiently.

Inventory turnover: $$\frac{\text{Cost of sales}}{\text{Inventories}}$$	Shows how rapidly a business's inventories are sold on average during the year
Inventory holding period (inventory days): $$\frac{\text{Inventories}}{\text{Cost of sales}} \times 365 \text{ days}$$	Average period for which a business holds an item of inventory
Trade receivables collection period: $$\frac{\text{Trade receivables}}{\text{Revenue}} \times 365 \text{ days}$$	Average period taken to collect receivables
Trade payables payment period: $$\frac{\text{Trade payables}}{\text{Cost of sales}} \times 365 \text{ days}$$	Average period taken to pay suppliers

Working capital cycle = Inventory days + Receivable days – Payable days

An increase in any of these periods can be a sign of liquidity problems

Financial position

Gearing: $\dfrac{\text{Non-current liabilities}}{\text{Total equity + Non-current liabilities}} \times 100\%$	This shows the extent to which a company is financed by debt (loan stock and/or other long term loans) rather than by equity (share capital and reserves).
Interest cover: $\dfrac{\text{Profit from operations}}{\text{Finance costs}}$	This shows whether a business is generating enough profit to meet its interest costs comfortably.

A company with a high gearing ratio often has low interest cover.

High gearing means that there is a greater risk to shareholders:

- Interest payments mean that less profit is available to pay dividends.
- Small changes in the level of operating profit can lead to big changes in the amount of profits available for dividends.

Main limitations

- Financial statements may be several months out of date.

- Financial statements only include information which can be measured in money terms; items such as intangible assets, human resources and reputation may have a significant effect on performance.

- Comparisons between businesses may be misleading:

    - Different accounting policies
    - Different markets/strategies
    - Effect of size

- Ratios may not always be calculated according to the same formula.

- Ratio analysis may be based on limited information.

Notes

Notes